JOSH STEVE

A Wealthy Heir's Mystery

Copyright © 2023 by Josh Steve

All rights reserved. No part of this publication may be reproduced, stored or transmitted in any form or by any means, electronic, mechanical, photocopying, recording, scanning, or otherwise without written permission from the publisher. It is illegal to copy this book, post it to a website, or distribute it by any other means without permission.

This novel is entirely a work of fiction. The names, characters and incidents portrayed in it are the work of the author's imagination. Any resemblance to actual persons, living or dead, events or localities is entirely coincidental.

Josh Steve asserts the moral right to be identified as the author of this work.

First edition

This book was professionally typeset on Reedsy.
Find out more at reedsy.com

Contents

The Inheritance	1
The Enigmatic Will	5
Family Secrets	9
The Disappearing Heirloom	14
The Haunting Night	19
The Confrontation	23
The Unfinished Business	26
The Legacy Unveiled	31
The Ghosts of Havenwood	35
The Unearthed Truth	38
The Final Confrontation	43
The Legacy's End	47

The Inheritance

The crimson sun dipped below the horizon, casting long shadows across the opulent estate. Its vast, manicured lawns stretched out like a sea of green velvet under the waning light. This was Havenwood Manor, an architectural masterpiece nestled amidst a dense forest, where secrets lay hidden beneath its stately facade. And at the center of it all stood Alexander Winters, a man whose life was about to be forever changed.

Alex's leather shoes crunched on the gravel driveway as he approached the imposing wrought-iron gates, their intricate patterns a stark contrast to the dense woods beyond. He checked his watch impatiently, his heart pounding with a mixture of anticipation and trepidation. His late grandfather, Victor Winters, had always been a mystery—a distant figure who'd never shown any particular affection for his only grandson. Yet, as Alex walked up the steps to the mansion, his mind whirled with curiosity about the cryptic message he'd received only days ago.

The doors to Havenwood Manor creaked open slowly, revealing a cavernous foyer bathed in dim, golden light. A chandelier hung from the ceiling, casting intricate patterns on the marble floor. Portraits of stern-faced ancestors lined the walls, their eyes following Alex's every step.

"Mr. Alexander Winters," a butler announced with a polite bow. "Welcome to

Havenwood Manor."

Alex nodded his thanks, unable to shake the feeling that he'd stepped into a different era. He followed the butler down a long corridor, the tap of their footsteps echoing eerily in the hushed mansion. The air was heavy with the scent of age, leather-bound books, and polished wood.

Finally, they reached a grand oak door adorned with a silver crest. The butler opened it, revealing a dimly lit study. Behind a massive mahogany desk sat a lawyer, a man named Mr. Thornton, who was Victor's longtime confidant.

"Please, have a seat, Mr. Winters," Mr. Thornton invited, gesturing to a plush leather chair. "We've been expecting you."

Alex took a seat, trying to hide his unease. The lawyer's face was a mask of professionalism, but there was something in his eyes, a glimmer of anticipation that made Alex's skin prickle.

"I'm sure you're wondering why you're here," Mr. Thornton began, his voice steady. "Your grandfather, Mr. Victor Winters, passed away recently. He left behind a rather unusual will."

Alex raised an eyebrow. Unusual was an understatement, considering Victor's enigmatic nature. He leaned forward, urging Mr. Thornton to continue.

"According to the terms of the will," Mr. Thornton explained, "you are to inherit the entirety of Havenwood Manor and its considerable fortune."

Alex's eyes widened in disbelief. The weight of the words hung in the air, and he struggled to process their meaning. He'd anticipated some inheritance, but the entirety of the estate? It was staggering.

"But there are conditions," Mr. Thornton continued, his voice taking on a somber tone. "Your grandfather was a man who valued secrets, Mr. Winters. He believed that true worth lay in uncovering the hidden truths of life."

Alex frowned, his curiosity piqued. "What conditions?"

Mr. Thornton produced a sealed envelope from his desk, emblazoned with Victor's wax seal. He slid it across the desk to Alex. "You are to open this envelope alone, and you must do so in the library at midnight, three days from now."

Alex took the envelope, his fingers trembling. The weight of the moment bore down on him, as if he were stepping into an elaborate riddle. "And if I don't?"

The lawyer's eyes bore into Alex's, and for the first time, he saw a hint of emotion in them—fear. "If you don't follow the instructions precisely, you will forfeit your inheritance, and Havenwood Manor will be lost to you forever."

Alex left the study, the envelope clutched tightly in his hand. As he wandered through the mansion's labyrinthine corridors, he couldn't shake the feeling that he was being watched. Shadows seemed to dance at the edge of his vision, and a chill crept down his spine.

Three days passed slowly, each moment filled with mounting tension. On the appointed night, the library was bathed in moonlight. The grand room was filled with towering shelves, their contents a testament to Victor's insatiable curiosity. Dust motes danced in the silver beams of light that filtered through the heavy curtains.

Alex stood before the fireplace, his breath shaky, as he carefully broke the wax seal on the envelope. Inside, he found a single sheet of paper, upon which were written Victor's final words:

"My dear Alexander,

In the heart of Havenwood Manor lies the truth you seek, the key to your inheritance. But it is not a path easily tread. Follow the riddles, embrace the secrets, and only then shall you unlock the legacy I leave behind.

Good luck, my heir.

Yours,
  Victor Winters"

With these cryptic words, Alex's journey into the depths of deception and inheritance had only just begun.

The Enigmatic Will

The moon hung low in the night sky, its pale glow seeping through the curtains of the library. Alex Winters stood before the fireplace, the letter from his late grandfather Victor clutched tightly in his hand. The words on the page echoed in his mind, leaving him with a sense of foreboding and anticipation. He was about to delve into a labyrinth of riddles, secrets, and, he feared, danger.

Taking a deep breath, Alex surveyed the room. The library was a sanctuary of knowledge, a vast expanse of towering bookshelves filled with ancient tomes, dusty encyclopedias, and leather-bound journals. It was here that his grandfather had spent countless hours, absorbed in his insatiable thirst for knowledge.

The cryptic letter had left Alex with more questions than answers. What truth was hidden within Havenwood Manor, and why had his grandfather chosen this elaborate way to reveal it? With resolve, he turned his attention to the bookshelves, searching for any clue or riddle that might lead him down the path Victor had set before him.

His fingers trailed over the spines of books, feeling for anything out of place. Hours passed, and frustration gnawed at him. He had discovered nothing but dusty volumes and ancient maps. It seemed as if the library held no answers, only more mysteries.

As midnight drew nearer, the room seemed to grow colder, and the air was thick with a sense of anticipation. Alex's gaze fell on a particularly ornate globe, positioned in a corner of the room. It looked out of place among the shelves of books. He approached it cautiously, turning it in his hands, and noticed that it spun on its axis with an unusual ease.

With a quick twist, the globe separated into two hemispheres, revealing a hollow interior. Inside, nestled among the velvet lining, was a small, aged leather-bound book. It was unlike any of the other books in the library, and its cover bore a mysterious symbol, a combination of arcane runes and celestial diagrams.

Alex's heart quickened as he opened the book, revealing handwritten pages filled with intricate diagrams and cryptic symbols. It was a journal, Victor's journal, and it appeared to be a record of his journey to uncover the secrets of Havenwood Manor.

The entries were filled with references to hidden passages, concealed compartments, and cryptic codes. Victor had been obsessed with unraveling the mysteries of the estate, and it was clear that this journal held the key to his grandfather's enigmatic will.

As Alex poured over the journal, he deciphered a series of clues that seemed to point to a specific location within the mansion. References to "the heart of Havenwood" and "where past meets future" hinted at a place Alex had explored as a child—the estate's sprawling clock tower.

With newfound determination, Alex set out on a quest to reach the clock tower, guided by the cryptic clues in his grandfather's journal. The mansion at night was a maze of shadows and whispers. Every creak of the floorboards and rustle of the curtains seemed to conspire against him.

As he ascended the winding staircase that led to the tower, the air grew colder, and a sense of unease settled over him. The towering clock faced him, its hands frozen in time. But there was something else—the sound of a faint, rhythmic ticking, unlike the usual mechanical workings of a clock.

Alex's heart pounded as he approached the clock. He remembered a childhood memory, his grandfather's words echoing in his mind: "The past meets the future." He examined the clock's face closely and noticed that one of the numbers, the number twelve, could be turned like a dial.

With trembling fingers, Alex rotated the number twelve to align with the current time—midnight. A soft click resonated through the tower, and a hidden compartment in the clock's base swung open, revealing a narrow spiral staircase leading even higher into the tower.

With the journal in hand, Alex climbed the stairs, each step echoing in the silence of the night. The spiral staircase seemed to go on forever, and the higher he climbed, the more disoriented he became. It was as if he were ascending into a different dimension altogether.

Finally, he emerged onto a small balcony at the top of the clock tower. The view was breathtaking—an expanse of moonlit forest stretched out beneath him, and the mansion itself appeared smaller, shrouded in darkness.

But there, on the balcony's stone floor, was a large wooden chest, ornate and ancient. It bore the same symbol as the journal. Alex knelt before it and slowly lifted the heavy lid, revealing a treasure trove of old documents, letters, and, most importantly, a sealed envelope.

The envelope was addressed to him, with the words "To My Heir" scrawled across the front in his grandfather's handwriting. With a mixture of excitement and trepidation, he broke the seal and withdrew the contents.

Inside was a second letter, another riddle from Victor:

"Alex,

You have taken the first step on this journey, but the path ahead is perilous. In the documents before you lies the truth about Havenwood Manor's history, my quest for knowledge, and the darkness that has plagued our family for generations.

Read them, for they hold the key to your destiny.

Yours,
  Victor Winters"

As Alex began to examine the documents, he realized that he was on the precipice of a revelation—one that would not only change his life but uncover the secrets that had haunted his family for generations. But what darkness lay within these pages, and what price would he pay for uncovering the truth.

Family Secrets

The early morning sun broke through the thick canopy of trees that surrounded Havenwood Manor, casting dappled shadows on the estate's grand facade. Alex Winters sat in the library, surrounded by a sea of documents and letters from the chest he had discovered in the clock tower. The night's revelations had left him with more questions than answers, and he was determined to uncover the truth about his family's dark history.

The documents before him were a labyrinth of names, dates, and obscure references. Among them, he found a series of letters exchanged between his grandfather, Victor, and a mysterious figure referred to only as "A. Blackwood." The letters hinted at a clandestine partnership, a shared obsession with the secrets of Havenwood Manor, and the lengths they were willing to go to uncover them.

As Alex delved deeper into the correspondence, he discovered that A. Blackwood had been involved in the acquisition of the estate decades ago. The transaction had been shrouded in secrecy, and it was clear that there was more to the story than met the eye. What had drawn Victor and Blackwood to this place, and what secrets had they been so desperate to uncover?

One particular letter, dated years before Alex was born, caught his attention. In it, Victor had written:

"Dear A. Blackwood,

The Manor conceals its truths with a malevolent glee. I have glimpsed its depths, felt the weight of its secrets, and I fear that I have unleashed a darkness that threatens to consume us all. We must tread carefully, for the past is a restless specter, and our pursuit of knowledge may have dire consequences.

Yours in trepidation,
   Victor Winters"

Alex's heart raced as he read those words. The ominous warning from his grandfather painted a chilling picture of Havenwood Manor as a place of malevolence and ancient secrets. He couldn't help but wonder if these secrets were the reason for his family's long history of misfortune and tragedy.

With newfound determination, Alex set out to uncover more about A. Blackwood. He searched through the documents for any clue that might reveal the identity of this mysterious figure. Among the letters, he found a reference to an old estate ledger that might contain more information.

The ledger was buried deep within the chest, covered in a layer of dust and age. As he flipped through its fragile pages, he discovered records of financial transactions related to the acquisition of Havenwood Manor. A name jumped out at him—Archibald Blackwood.

Archibald Blackwood had been the owner of the estate before Victor, and it appeared that the transfer of ownership had been far from ordinary. A series of entries detailed large sums of money changing hands, but the purpose of these transactions remained unclear. What had Victor paid for, and what had Blackwood gained?

Alex's curiosity grew as he continued to read. He unearthed a faded photograph tucked between the pages of the ledger—a photograph of Victor and Archibald standing together in front of the clock tower. Their expressions were somber, as if they were burdened by the weight of their secrets.

The pieces of the puzzle were coming together, but there was still much to uncover. What had Victor and Blackwood been searching for within Havenwood Manor? And what had driven them to such lengths to acquire it?

As the morning turned to afternoon, Alex decided it was time to seek answers beyond the confines of the library. He knew that his family held its own share of secrets, and it was time to confront them. He made his way to the family wing of the mansion, where his parents, Amelia and Edward Winters, resided.

The corridor leading to their chambers was adorned with portraits of Winters ancestors, each face etched with the same air of mystery and solemnity. Alex had always been told that their family had a long and storied history, but the details had always been kept from him.

He knocked on the ornate door to his parents' chambers, and it swung open to reveal his mother, Amelia, a woman of grace and elegance who had always carried herself with an air of aloofness. Her eyes widened in surprise at the sight of her son.

"Alex? What brings you here?" she asked, her tone a mixture of curiosity and unease.

"I need answers, Mom," Alex replied, his voice determined. "Answers about this place, about our family, and about the secrets that have haunted us for generations."

Amelia hesitated for a moment before stepping aside, allowing Alex to enter the dimly lit chamber. Edward Winters, his father, sat at a grand desk cluttered with papers. He looked up, his expression guarded.

"What's this all about, Alex?" Edward inquired, his voice tinged with caution.

Alex wasted no time. He shared the contents of the letters and the ledger he had discovered, explaining the ominous warning from his grandfather and the enigmatic partnership with A. Blackwood. The room grew heavy with tension as he spoke, and the weight of the family secrets hung in the air.

Amelia and Edward exchanged glances, their faces etched with a mixture of guilt and resignation. It was clear that they had been keeping their own secrets, and the time for secrecy had come to an end.

Finally, Amelia spoke, her voice barely above a whisper. "Havenwood Manor is not what it seems, Alex. Your grandfather and Archibald Blackwood were drawn to it by forces beyond their control. They believed that the estate held the key to unlocking ancient powers, powers that could change the course of history."

Edward added, "But with those powers came great danger. We've lived under the shadow of those secrets for years, trying to protect you from the darkness that lurks within this place."

Alex's mind raced as he processed their words. The revelations were both bewildering and terrifying. He had always thought of Havenwood Manor as a place of opulence and privilege, but now it appeared to be a place of ancient mysteries and malevolence.

"What did they find?" Alex asked, his voice trembling. "What is the truth about this estate?"

Amelia glanced at her husband, her eyes filled with sorrow. "We don't know, Alex. Victor and Archibald disappeared without a trace, leaving us with fragments of their research and a legacy of fear."

As the weight of his family's legacy settled on his shoulders, Alex realized that he was not only on a journey to uncover the truth but also to confront the darkness that had plagued his family for generations. The secrets of Havenwood Manor ran deep, and he was determined to unearth them, no matter the cost.

The Disappearing Heirloom

Days turned into weeks as Alex Winters delved deeper into the mysteries of Havenwood Manor. The revelations about his grandfather's involvement with Archibald Blackwood and their pursuit of ancient powers weighed heavily on his mind. But there was more to uncover, and the estate held its secrets close, like a jealous guardian.

One chilly evening, as the sun dipped below the horizon and the estate's grand windows cast elongated shadows across the polished wooden floors, Alex found himself in the heart of the mansion—the opulent dining room. He had learned from his grandfather's journal that this room was more than a place for lavish feasts; it held a connection to the hidden truths of Havenwood.

Alex had spent hours examining every inch of the dining room, from the towering chandelier to the intricately carved dining table. But it was a particular heirloom that had captured his attention—a magnificent silver candelabrum adorned with intricate filigree and delicate crystal drops. It had been a fixture of the dining room for generations, passed down through the Winters family.

According to Victor's journal, the candelabrum was more than just a piece of ornate decoration. It was rumored to hold a hidden compartment, a place where Victor had stashed away crucial documents and artifacts related to his quest for knowledge. This was the lead that could bring him closer to uncovering the true nature of the estate's secrets.

With a sense of anticipation, Alex examined the candelabrum. It stood tall and imposing, a relic from a bygone era. His fingers traced the delicate patterns of the silver, searching for any sign of a concealed compartment. His grandfather's journal contained vague references to a hidden latch, but finding it proved to be a daunting task.

The minutes stretched into hours as Alex meticulously examined the candelabrum, his mind racing to decipher the clues left behind by his grandfather. Frustration threatened to overtake him, but he refused to give up. The secrets of Havenwood Manor were within his reach, and he couldn't afford to falter now.

Then, as his fingers grazed a particularly ornate section of the candelabrum's base, he felt a subtle indentation—a hidden groove that seemed out of place. With bated breath, he pressed it, and a soft click resonated through the room.

The candelabrum shifted, revealing a hidden compartment beneath its base. Alex carefully lifted the compartment's lid, revealing a trove of artifacts, letters, and a leather-bound journal. It was Victor's handwriting once again, chronicling his discoveries and descent into the darkness of the estate's secrets.

The journal entries were filled with references to an ancient ritual, one that could unlock the true potential of Havenwood Manor. Victor believed that the candelabrum held the key to this ritual, a ritual that involved the alignment of celestial events and the unlocking of the estate's hidden powers.

Alex's heart raced as he read the entries. It seemed that the candelabrum was more than just a family heirloom; it was a conduit to ancient forces that had eluded his grandfather and Archibald Blackwood. But the ritual was dangerous, and the consequences of failure were dire.

As Alex contemplated his next steps, a strange noise echoed through the dining room—a soft, almost imperceptible hum. He turned toward the source of the sound, his eyes widening in astonishment. The candelabrum, which had been a fixture of the room for centuries, was slowly levitating into the air, its crystal drops shimmering in the dim light.

Fear and awe warred within Alex as he watched the candelabrum hover, its filigree patterns casting intricate shadows on the walls. It was as if the candelabrum itself was responding to the knowledge he had uncovered, and the realization sent shivers down his spine.

Suddenly, the candelabrum began to spin, its crystal drops creating a mesmerizing kaleidoscope of colors. It spun faster and faster, and a strange vortex formed above it—an otherworldly portal that seemed to defy the laws of physics. Alex watched in awe as the portal expanded, revealing a glimpse of an ethereal realm beyond.

With a burst of courage, Alex reached out and touched the portal, his fingers passing through the shimmering barrier. It felt like cool silk against his skin. The room around him seemed to blur, and he was drawn into the portal, his world spiraling into a surreal dreamscape.

In this otherworldly realm, Alex found himself in a vast library, its shelves stretching endlessly into the distance. The air was filled with the scent of ancient parchment, and the books whispered secrets that only he could hear. He realized that he had entered the very heart of Havenwood's mysteries, a place where knowledge and magic converged.

As he wandered through the spectral library, he discovered more journals, more artifacts, and the remnants of the ritual that Victor had desperately sought to complete. The entries in the journals hinted at the dangers of meddling with ancient forces, the toll it had taken on Victor's sanity, and the ever-present threat that loomed over the estate.

But the most startling discovery lay at the center of the library—a massive tome bound in black leather. Its pages were filled with incantations, diagrams, and forbidden knowledge. It was the culmination of Victor's quest, a book that held the key to unlocking the true power of Havenwood Manor.

With trepidation, Alex reached for the book, his fingers brushing its pages. He could feel the weight of its dark magic, the pull of a destiny that had been set into motion long before his birth. He knew that the decisions he made in that moment would determine the fate of the estate, his family, and himself.

As he opened the book, a surge of energy coursed through him, and the very fabric of the otherworldly library seemed to tremble. The words on the pages were incomprehensible, yet he felt an innate understanding of their meaning. The ancient ritual, the alignment of celestial events, and the candelabrum—all converged in that moment.

With resolve, Alex began to chant the incantation, his voice echoing through the spectral library. The room itself seemed to respond, the books whispering their approval. The ritual had begun, and the estate's hidden powers surged to life.

But with power came danger. As the ritual neared its culmination, the very foundations of the library shook, and a shadowy presence emerged from the darkness. It was a malevolent force, a guardian of the estate's secrets, and it sought to thwart Alex's efforts.

A battle of wills ensued as Alex struggled to complete the ritual, his determination pitted against the ancient darkness. The spectral library became a battleground, its shelves collapsing, and its books swirling in a chaotic dance. The fate of Havenwood Manor hung in the balance, and the outcome was far from certain.

With a final surge of strength, Alex uttered the last words of the incantation, and a blinding light engulfed the library. The force of the magic sent him hurtling back through the portal, and he emerged in the dining room, gasping for breath.

The candelabrum had returned to its rightful place, no longer hovering in the air. The room bore no sign of the otherworldly journey he had undertaken, but the knowledge he had gained and the power he had harnessed lingered within him.

The

secrets of Havenwood Manor had been unlocked, and the estate's hidden powers were now at his disposal. But with that power came the responsibility to confront the malevolent forces that lurked within, forces that had haunted his family for generations. The darkness had been unleashed, and the battle for the legacy of Havenwood had only just begun.

The Haunting Night

The moon hung low in the midnight sky, casting an eerie glow over Havenwood Manor. Alex Winters stood in the center of the dining room, the candelabrum before him, its crystal drops refracting the pale moonlight. He had unlocked the estate's hidden powers, but with that power came a sense of unease—a feeling that he was not alone in the mansion.

The events of the otherworldly library had left him with a deeper understanding of the secrets that lay within Havenwood. The ancient ritual he had performed had tapped into the estate's magic, revealing hidden knowledge and potential. But it had also awakened something darker, something that now lurked in the shadows.

As Alex contemplated his next steps, a soft whisper echoed through the room, a haunting melody that seemed to emanate from nowhere and everywhere at once. It sent a shiver down his spine, and he realized that the mansion itself was alive with an otherworldly presence.

The whispering continued, growing louder and more insistent, as if beckoning him to follow. It led him through the grand corridors of the mansion, its voice filled with a melancholic yearning. Alex couldn't resist its pull, and he moved with an almost trance-like determination.

He found himself in the mansion's vast, dimly lit foyer, where the moonlight filtered through the stained-glass windows, casting a mosaic of colors on the marble floor. The whispering led him toward a grand staircase, its ornate banisters adorned with intricate carvings.

With each step, the presence seemed to grow stronger, and Alex's heart pounded in his chest. He knew that he was on the verge of a revelation, one that would bring him closer to uncovering the true nature of Havenwood Manor.

At the top of the staircase, he entered a long corridor that seemed to stretch endlessly. The walls were lined with portraits of long-dead ancestors, their eyes following his every move. The whispering guided him to a massive oak door at the end of the corridor—a door that seemed to pulse with an otherworldly energy.

With a sense of trepidation, Alex pushed open the door and entered a room that defied the laws of space and time. It was a vast, ethereal chamber filled with swirling mists and shimmering lights. Shadows danced on the walls, and a haunting melody echoed through the space.

In the center of the chamber stood a spectral figure—a woman dressed in an elegant gown of another era, her hair cascading in waves around her shoulders. Her eyes were pools of darkness, and her presence exuded an otherworldly beauty and sadness.

"Welcome, Alexander," the woman's voice echoed in his mind, a voice that seemed to be both a whisper and a wail.

Alex could barely find his voice as he addressed the apparition. "Who are you?"

The woman's form wavered, as if struggling to maintain her presence. "I am

Isabella Winters, a soul bound to this estate for centuries. I am both protector and prisoner, trapped by the darkness that haunts Havenwood."

Isabella's words sent a chill through Alex. She was a Winters ancestor, a guardian of the estate, and yet she spoke of being trapped. He couldn't help but ask, "What darkness haunts this place? What is its connection to my family?"

Isabella's form flickered, and she seemed to grow weaker. "The darkness is a malevolent force, a curse that has plagued the Winters bloodline for generations. It is born of the pursuit of power and knowledge, a thirst that led to the creation of Havenwood Manor. But the curse demands a price—a price that has been paid with the suffering of our family."

As she spoke, images flashed before Alex's eyes—his ancestors, tormented by visions and madness, their lives marked by tragedy and despair. It was a legacy of suffering that he had only begun to comprehend.

"The darkness seeks to consume the living," Isabella continued, her voice trembling. "It feeds on the fear and ambition of those who enter this estate. But you, Alexander, have the power to confront it, to break the cycle of suffering. You hold the key to Havenwood's salvation."

Alex's mind raced as he grappled with the enormity of his task. He had unlocked the estate's hidden powers, but now he realized that he must confront the malevolent force that had plagued his family for generations. The haunting melodies and whispers of the mansion were manifestations of the darkness, and it was time to face the source of the curse.

Isabella extended a spectral hand toward him, her eyes filled with an unspoken plea. "Embrace the power within you, Alexander. Confront the darkness and free our family from its grasp. The candelabrum you unlocked is the key to sealing the curse, but the ritual must be completed. Only then can

Havenwood be cleansed."

With determination burning in his veins, Alex nodded. He knew that he couldn't turn away from the responsibility that had been thrust upon him. He had the knowledge, the power, and the legacy of his family to guide him.

As Isabella's form faded back into the mists, she left him with a final haunting melody—a melody that seemed to resonate in his very soul. It was a call to action, a reminder of the suffering that had endured for too long within Havenwood Manor.

With newfound resolve, Alex retraced his steps through the spectral chamber, down the grand staircase, and back to the dining room. He knew that the darkness awaited him, but he was armed with knowledge and purpose. The battle for the legacy of Havenwood had reached its climax, and the haunting night was far from over.

The Confrontation

The grand dining room of Havenwood Manor was cloaked in a hushed stillness, save for the flickering candlelight that cast long, wavering shadows on the walls. Alex Winters stood before the candelabrum, the silver heirloom that had been both a source of power and a harbinger of darkness. He had uncovered the truth about the curse that had plagued his family for generations, and now it was time to confront the malevolent force that lurked within the estate.

As he gazed at the candelabrum, its crystal drops glinting like frozen tears, he couldn't help but think of the haunting figure of Isabella Winters—the guardian and prisoner of Havenwood. Her spectral presence had revealed the curse's origins and the dire consequences of the pursuit of power and knowledge.

With a deep breath, Alex approached the candelabrum, his fingers trembling as he recalled the ritual described in his grandfather's journal. The incantation, the alignment of celestial events—it was all part of a complex process to harness the estate's magic and seal the curse. The daunting task loomed before him, and he knew that the battle for Havenwood's legacy would be waged on this very night.

The room seemed to respond to his presence, as if the mansion itself were aware of the impending confrontation. The haunting melodies and whispers grew louder, swirling around him like a tempest of sound. It was as if the darkness within the estate was aware of his intentions and sought to thwart his every move.

With a steely resolve, Alex began the ritual, his voice trembling as he chanted the incantation. The words flowed from his lips like a river of magic, and the candelabrum began to levitate once more, its crystal drops shimmering with an otherworldly light. The room quivered, and the very air seemed to vibrate with power.

But this time, the malevolent force that had haunted his family for generations did not remain hidden in the shadows. As the ritual progressed, a darkness began to coalesce around the candelabrum—a swirling, amorphous mass that seemed to draw upon the very essence of the mansion itself.

Alex's heart pounded as he continued the incantation, his voice filled with determination. He could feel the malevolent force resisting, a malevolence that sought to consume him and everything he held dear. It whispered promises of power, of forbidden knowledge, and it was a seductive lure that threatened to ensnare his soul.

The battle of wills raged on, and the room trembled as the darkness pushed back against the light of the ritual. Shadows danced on the walls, and the spectral melodies grew discordant, as if the very fabric of reality was tearing apart.

Then, with a final surge of energy, Alex uttered the last words of the incantation, and a blinding light erupted from the candelabrum. The force of the magic sent him staggering backward, and he shielded his eyes from the blinding radiance.

As the light began to fade, Alex opened his eyes and saw that the malevolent force had been banished. The swirling darkness dissipated, leaving only a sense of emptiness in its wake. The candelabrum, once a conduit for the curse, had been transformed into a beacon of pure light.

Alex knew that the curse had been sealed, and a weight had been lifted from the estate. But he also knew that the darkness would not give up easily. It had been vanquished for now, but it would forever be a lurking presence, waiting for an opportunity to return.

With a weary sigh, Alex stepped away from the candelabrum, its crystal drops now gleaming with an ethereal radiance. He knew that his family's legacy was no longer bound by the curse, but the haunting melodies and whispers that echoed through the mansion served as a constant reminder of the darkness that had once gripped Havenwood.

As he left the dining room, he couldn't help but wonder what lay ahead for him and the estate. The battle for the legacy of Havenwood had been won, but the war against the malevolent force was far from over. The secrets of the mansion were buried deep, and the darkness would continue to haunt the Winters family, awaiting the next heir who would be drawn into its web of mystery and malevolence.

The grand dining room fell silent once more, its flickering candles casting long, wavering shadows on the walls. The candelabrum stood as a testament to the enduring power of the estate, a beacon of light in the heart of darkness— a symbol of hope for the future of Havenwood Manor.

The Unfinished Business

Days turned into weeks after the confrontation with the malevolent force that had haunted Havenwood Manor for generations. The mansion itself seemed to breathe a sigh of relief, its oppressive atmosphere lifting, and the haunting melodies and whispers growing fainter with each passing day.

Alex Winters had taken on the role of guardian of the estate's secrets, a duty he had not asked for but had accepted with determination. He had sealed the curse that had plagued his family, but he knew that the darkness was not entirely vanquished. It lingered on the periphery, waiting for an opportunity to return.

The candelabrum, transformed into a beacon of light, remained in the dining room as a constant reminder of the malevolent force that had once held the mansion in its grip. Its crystal drops still shimmered with an ethereal radiance, a testament to the power that Alex had harnessed to confront the curse.

But despite the temporary peace that had settled over Havenwood, there was a sense of unfinished business—a lingering mystery that refused to be ignored. The secrets of the estate still called out to him, a siren's song that beckoned him to delve deeper into the darkness that had once consumed his family.

One evening, as the sun dipped below the horizon and the mansion was bathed in the soft glow of twilight, Alex found himself drawn to the clock tower—a place that had been at the center of his grandfather's quest for knowledge. The journal that Victor had left behind contained cryptic references to the tower, and Alex knew that there was more to uncover.

The winding staircase that led to the clock tower seemed to stretch endlessly, and the air grew colder with each step. Alex ascended with a sense of trepidation, the memory of his previous journey to the tower still fresh in his mind. He couldn't help but wonder what new revelations awaited him.

As he reached the top of the tower, he emerged onto the balcony, the same balcony where he had discovered the chest of documents and the sealed envelope from his grandfather. The moon hung low in the sky, casting a silvery glow over the estate, and the mansion itself appeared smaller, shrouded in darkness.

But this time, the balcony revealed something new—a hidden compartment in the stone floor, obscured by a thick layer of dust and age. It was a discovery that sent a jolt of excitement through Alex, for he knew that it held the key to the estate's remaining secrets.

With careful fingers, he opened the compartment, revealing a leather-bound journal that bore his grandfather's unmistakable handwriting. It was a continuation of Victor's previous journal, chronicling his quest to uncover the true nature of Havenwood and the curse that had plagued their family.

The entries were filled with references to ancient rituals, hidden passages, and the existence of an underground chamber deep beneath the mansion—an chamber that had remained hidden for centuries. Victor believed that this chamber held the final pieces of the puzzle, the key to fully understanding the estate's mysteries.

With newfound determination, Alex retraced his steps through the clock tower and descended to the mansion below. He knew that he had to find the entrance to the underground chamber, to uncover the secrets that had eluded his grandfather and Archibald Blackwood.

The clues in the journal led him to the library, where he examined the books and manuscripts that lined the shelves. Victor's entries hinted at a particular book that held the key to unlocking the passage to the underground chamber. It was a book of arcane symbols and ancient knowledge, and it was said to be the key to accessing the hidden depths of Havenwood.

After hours of searching, Alex finally found the book—a dusty tome with a cover adorned with cryptic symbols. As he opened it, he realized that the pages were filled with intricate diagrams and incantations that seemed to resonate with the magic of the estate.

With the book in hand, Alex retraced his steps once more, this time to the grand library, where Victor's journal had hinted at a hidden mechanism that would reveal the entrance to the underground chamber. He examined the room with a meticulous eye, searching for any sign of a concealed passage.

Then, as he approached the fireplace, he noticed something unusual—a series of symbols etched into the stone hearth. They matched the diagrams in the book he held. With a sense of anticipation, he touched the symbols in the order described in the journal, and a low rumble filled the room.

The stone hearth began to shift, revealing a hidden staircase that descended into darkness. The air grew colder, and the sense of unease that had lingered within the mansion returned with a vengeance. But Alex knew that he had to press forward, to uncover the final secrets of Havenwood.

As he descended the narrow staircase, the walls seemed to close in around him, and the air grew heavy with the weight of centuries-old secrets. The staircase seemed to stretch endlessly, and the darkness threatened to consume him. But he pressed on, driven by a relentless determination to uncover the truth.

Finally, he emerged into an underground chamber—a vast, cavernous space that seemed to defy the laws of physics. The walls were adorned with ancient symbols and illuminated by an otherworldly glow. In the center of the chamber stood a stone pedestal, upon which rested a book—a book that radiated with a malevolent energy.

With a sense of foreboding, Alex approached the pedestal and opened the book. Its pages were filled with incantations and diagrams that seemed to pulsate with dark magic. It was a book of forbidden knowledge, a tome that held the secrets of the malevolent force that had plagued his family.

As he read the incantations aloud, the chamber itself seemed to come alive, the symbols on the walls glowing with an eerie light. Shadows danced on the stone floor, and a sense of dread filled the air. Alex realized that he had stumbled upon a source of great power, one that had the potential to unleash the darkness once more.

With a sinking feeling, he closed the book and backed away from the pedestal. He knew that the only way to protect his family and the legacy of Havenwood was to seal the book away, to ensure that its forbidden knowledge could never be used again.

As he left the underground chamber and ascended the narrow staircase, he felt a profound sense of unease. The secrets of Havenwood were vast and complex, and the darkness that lurked within the estate was a force that would forever haunt his family.

The mansion itself seemed to hold its breath, as if waiting for the next heir who would be drawn into its web of mystery and malevolence. The unfinished business of Havenwood would always linger, a reminder that the battle for its legacy was never truly over.

The Legacy Unveiled

The darkened corridors of Havenwood Manor seemed to close in around Alex Winters as he made his way back to the grand library. The weight of the secrets he had uncovered bore heavily on his shoulders, and the unsettling knowledge of the malevolent force that still lurked within the estate gnawed at his mind.

His encounter with the underground chamber had revealed the depths of the darkness that had plagued his family for generations. The book of forbidden knowledge he had discovered held the key to unleashing that darkness once more, and it was a power that could not be allowed to fall into the wrong hands.

As he entered the grand library, he knew that he had to find a way to safeguard the book, to ensure that it could never be used to resurrect the malevolent force. The journal left behind by his grandfather, Victor, contained clues that hinted at a hidden compartment within the library—one that held the key to protecting Havenwood's legacy.

The search was painstaking, as Alex meticulously examined every inch of the room. The walls were adorned with shelves of books and manuscripts, each one a repository of knowledge and mystery. It was a place where the past and the present converged, and the air was thick with the scent of ancient parchment.

Then, as he moved a heavy wooden bookshelf aside, he noticed something unusual—a faint outline of a doorway hidden behind the shelves. With a sense of anticipation, he pushed against the wall, and it swung open to reveal a hidden chamber.

The chamber was small and dimly lit, its walls lined with shelves that held a collection of books, scrolls, and artifacts. In the center of the room stood a pedestal, upon which rested a stone box adorned with intricate carvings. It was the very box that Victor had mentioned in his journal—a box that held the key to safeguarding the book of forbidden knowledge.

As Alex approached the stone box, he could feel the weight of history pressing down upon him. It was a relic from a bygone era, a testament to the lengths his ancestors had gone to protect the secrets of Havenwood. He knew that he had to unlock the box, to ensure that the book was sealed away for all time.

With careful fingers, he examined the carvings on the box, searching for any sign of a hidden mechanism. It took several tense moments of trial and error, but finally, he discovered a concealed latch. With a soft click, the box opened, revealing the book of forbidden knowledge.

As he gazed at the book, its pages filled with dark incantations and symbols, he couldn't help but feel a sense of unease. It was a tome of unimaginable power, and the malevolent force it represented was a specter that haunted his family's legacy. But he knew that sealing it away was the only option.

With determination burning in his veins, he placed the book inside the stone box and closed it once more. The sense of relief was palpable, as if the very room itself exhaled in relief. The book of forbidden knowledge was now sealed away, safeguarded from those who would seek to harness its dark magic.

But as Alex stepped away from the stone box, a sense of foreboding settled over him. He knew that the malevolent force still lurked within the estate, waiting for an opportunity to return. The secrets of Havenwood were vast and complex, and the darkness that haunted the mansion was a legacy that could not be easily dispelled.

As he left the hidden chamber and made his way through the grand library, he couldn't help but wonder what lay ahead for him and the estate. The battle for Havenwood's legacy was a never-ending struggle, one that would persist for generations to come.

The mansion itself seemed to whisper its secrets, its walls echoing with the stories of those who had walked its grand corridors. It was a place of opulence and mystery, a place where the past and the present converged in a never-ending dance.

As he emerged from the grand library and made his way through the moonlit corridors, he realized that his journey was far from over. The legacy of Havenwood would continue to haunt him, a reminder that the battle against the darkness was a battle that could never truly be won.

But he also knew that he was now the guardian of the estate's secrets, the protector of his family's legacy. It was a responsibility he had accepted with open eyes, knowing that the secrets of Havenwood were a burden he would carry for the rest of his days.

The night outside was quiet, the moon casting a silvery glow over the mansion's grand facade. Alex stood for a moment, gazing up at the clock tower, where his journey had begun. It was a place of mystery and malevolence, a place where the past and the present converged.

With a sense of determination, he turned and made his way back into the heart of Havenwood Manor. The legacy of the estate would continue to reveal its secrets, and the darkness that haunted it would remain a relentless presence. But he was ready to confront whatever challenges lay ahead, to protect the mansion and his family's name from the malevolent force that had haunted them for generations.

The Ghosts of Havenwood

Havenwood Manor had fallen into a profound silence. The malevolent force that had haunted the estate for generations had been sealed away, and the haunting melodies and whispers that had once filled its corridors had grown faint. But within the mansion's opulent walls, a different kind of silence had settled—a silence that was pregnant with the weight of history and secrets.

Alex Winters had become the guardian of those secrets, a role he had accepted with solemn determination. The book of forbidden knowledge that held the key to unleashing the darkness had been sealed within a hidden chamber in the grand library, safeguarded from those who might seek to wield its power. Yet, despite the temporary peace that had descended upon Havenwood, Alex knew that the malevolent force still lingered, waiting for an opportunity to return.

As he walked the grand corridors of the mansion, his footsteps echoing in the silence, he couldn't help but feel the presence of something otherworldly—a sense that the past and the present were intertwined in ways he could scarcely comprehend. The weight of his family's legacy bore heavily upon him, and the knowledge that the battle against the darkness was far from over weighed on his mind.

It was on one particularly chilly evening, as he stood before the ornate mirror in his grandfather's old study, that he felt a strange sensation—a prickling at the nape of his neck, as if he were being watched. He turned toward the room, his heart quickening as he realized that he was not alone.

Standing in the dimly lit study was a figure—a spectral presence that seemed to flicker in and out of existence. It was a woman, her form ethereal and translucent, her eyes pools of darkness. She bore an uncanny resemblance to Isabella Winters, the guardian and prisoner of Havenwood.

"Who are you?" Alex whispered, his voice trembling with a mixture of fear and curiosity.

The spectral woman regarded him with a mournful expression, her voice a haunting echo. "I am Eleanor Winters, a soul bound to this estate for centuries, like Isabella before me. We are both protectors and prisoners of Havenwood."

Alex's mind reeled as he realized that he was face to face with another ancestor, another guardian of the mansion. "What do you seek, Eleanor?"

Eleanor's form flickered, as if struggling to maintain her presence. "I seek to warn you, Alexander. The darkness has not been fully banished. It lingers in the shadows, waiting for an opportunity to return. You must be vigilant."

Alex nodded, his determination resolute. "I know that the battle is not over. I will do whatever it takes to protect my family and the legacy of Havenwood."

Eleanor's spectral form seemed to waver, as if she were fading away. "You carry a heavy burden, Alexander, as we all have. The secrets of this estate run deep, and the darkness is a relentless force. But you have the power to confront it, to ensure that our family's suffering is not in vain."

With those words, Eleanor's presence dissipated, leaving the study in silence once more. Alex knew that he had been given a warning, a reminder that the malevolent force that had plagued his family would always be a lurking presence, waiting for an opportunity to return.

As he left the study and made his way through the mansion, he couldn't shake the feeling that he was not alone—that the ghosts of Havenwood were watching, waiting, and whispering their secrets in the silence.

His journey had only just begun, and the legacy of the estate continued to reveal its mysteries. The malevolent force that had haunted the mansion would remain a relentless presence, but Alex was ready to confront whatever challenges lay ahead.

The night outside was dark and still, the moon hidden behind a shroud of clouds. Havenwood Manor stood as a sentinel in the darkness, a place of opulence and mystery, where the past and the present converged in an eternal dance.

With determination burning in his veins, Alex stepped forward into the heart of the mansion. The ghosts of Havenwood whispered their secrets in the silence, and the battle for the legacy of the estate would persist for generations to come.

The Unearthed Truth

The moon hung low in the night sky, casting a silvery glow over Havenwood Manor. The mansion, steeped in history and secrets, stood in solemn silence, its grand facade cloaked in shadows. Alex Winters, the guardian of his family's legacy, could not escape the feeling that the malevolent force that had plagued his ancestors still lingered within the estate.

Restless and driven by an unquenchable curiosity, Alex had been spending countless hours in the grand library, poring over the books, scrolls, and manuscripts that lined the shelves. His grandfather's journal had hinted at even deeper layers of mystery within the mansion—layers that went beyond the book of forbidden knowledge he had sealed away.

As he scanned the ancient tomes and artifacts, he couldn't help but wonder if there were more hidden chambers, more secrets buried beneath the opulent surface of Havenwood. He had to know the truth, to uncover the full extent of the malevolent force that had haunted his family.

It was during one of these late-night investigations that he stumbled upon a seemingly inconspicuous book—a weathered leather-bound volume titled "Havenwood: A Chronicle of Secrets." The book bore no author's name, and its pages were filled with handwritten entries, detailing the history of the estate and the darkness that had plagued it.

With a sense of anticipation, Alex began to read. The entries dated back centuries, chronicling the Winters family's connection to Havenwood and the malevolent force that had become intertwined with their bloodline. It was a chilling account of tragedy, madness, and despair—a legacy that had endured for generations.

As he delved deeper into the book, he discovered references to hidden passages and chambers within the mansion—passages that had remained undiscovered for centuries. The entries spoke of a secret underground network of tunnels that crisscrossed beneath Havenwood, connecting various parts of the estate.

One entry, in particular, caught Alex's attention. It mentioned a hidden chamber deep beneath the clock tower—the very same clock tower where his journey had begun. According to the chronicle, this chamber held the darkest secrets of Havenwood and was a place of great power.

Driven by an insatiable curiosity and a burning need to confront the malevolent force once and for all, Alex decided to search for the entrance to the hidden chamber beneath the clock tower. Armed with a lantern and a sense of purpose, he made his way through the moonlit corridors of the mansion.

The clock tower, with its imposing presence, seemed to beckon him. The winding staircase that led to its upper levels appeared unchanged from his previous visits, but he knew that there was more to discover. He ascended the steps with determination, his lantern casting flickering shadows on the walls.

As he reached the top of the tower, he emerged onto the familiar balcony. The moon bathed the estate in a silvery light, and the night air was cool and crisp. But this time, he was not content to simply gaze at the mansion's grand facade. He was on a mission to uncover the truth that lay hidden beneath.

With a careful eye, he examined the balcony's stone floor, searching for any sign of a concealed entrance. Then, he noticed it—a faint seam in the stone, barely visible in the dim light. It was the entrance to the hidden chamber.

With a sense of anticipation and trepidation, he pushed against the stone floor, and it gave way with a soft rumble. The staircase that led downward was steep and narrow, and the air grew colder with each step. He descended into the depths of Havenwood, lantern in hand, the shadows closing in around him.

Finally, he emerged into a vast underground chamber, its walls adorned with the same intricate symbols and carvings he had seen in his grandfather's journal. The chamber was illuminated by an otherworldly glow, and the air was heavy with a sense of foreboding.

In the center of the chamber stood a stone pedestal, upon which rested a book—a book that radiated with dark energy. It was the same book of forbidden knowledge he had sealed away in the hidden chamber of the grand library. It seemed that the malevolent force had found a way to resurrect itself.

With a sinking feeling, Alex realized that the battle was far from over. The darkness had returned, and it had taken root in the very heart of Havenwood. He knew that he had to confront it, to banish it once and for all.

As he approached the stone pedestal, he felt a malevolent presence enveloping him—a force that sought to ensnare his mind and soul. The book opened of its own accord, its pages filled with dark incantations and symbols that pulsed with malevolent power.

With determination burning in his veins, Alex knew that he had to fight back. He began to chant a counter-incantation, one that he had uncovered in the chronicle of secrets—a chant that was meant to bind the darkness and banish it from the estate.

The chamber trembled, and the symbols on the walls glowed with an eerie light. Shadows danced on the stone floor, and the malevolent force lashed out with a furious intensity. But Alex continued to chant, his voice unwavering, his will unbroken.

As the battle of wills raged on, Alex could feel the darkness weakening, its grip on the mansion loosening. The book of forbidden knowledge began to close, its pages turning with an otherworldly force, and the malevolent presence retreated.

With a final surge of energy, Alex uttered the last words of the counter-incantation, and the chamber was filled with blinding light. The force of the magic sent him staggering backward, and he shielded his eyes from the radiance.

When the light finally faded, he opened his eyes to see that the darkness had been banished once more. The book of forbidden knowledge lay closed on the stone pedestal, its dark power vanquished. The malevolent force had been driven from Havenwood.

As he left the underground chamber and ascended the narrow staircase, he felt a profound sense of relief. The battle against the darkness had been won once again, but he knew that the malevolent force would always be a lurking presence, waiting for an opportunity to return.

The mansion itself seemed to exhale in relief, as if the very walls were aware of the victory. The secrets of Havenwood were vast and complex, and the darkness that had once haunted the estate would forever be a part of its legacy.

With a weary but resolute heart, Alex made his way through the moonlit corridors of the mansion. The legacy of Havenwood would continue to reveal its mysteries, and the battle against the malevolent force would persist for generations to come.

The night outside was quiet, the moon casting a silvery glow over the grand facade of Havenwood Manor. Alex stood for a moment, gazing up at the clock tower, where his journey had taken him once more. It was a place of mystery and malevolence, where the past and the present converged.

With a sense of determination, he turned and made his way back into the heart of Havenwood. The ghosts of the mansion had whispered their secrets in the silence, and the legacy of the estate would continue to unfold, one revelation at a time.

The Final Confrontation

The dawn broke over Havenwood Manor, its golden light casting a serene glow over the mansion's grand facade. It was a new day, and a sense of calm had settled over the estate. The malevolent force that had haunted the Winters family for generations had been banished once more, and the haunting melodies and whispers that had filled its corridors had grown faint.

But within the opulent walls of the mansion, a tension lingered—a tension that hinted at an unfinished battle, a lingering darkness that refused to be extinguished. Alex Winters, the guardian of his family's legacy, knew that the malevolent force still lurked, waiting for an opportunity to return.

After the harrowing encounter in the underground chamber beneath the clock tower, Alex had been relentless in his pursuit of answers. The book of forbidden knowledge had been sealed away once more, but he couldn't escape the feeling that there were deeper layers of mystery within Havenwood that had yet to be uncovered.

His grandfather's journal had hinted at a hidden chamber deep within the mansion—a chamber that held the darkest secrets of Havenwood. It was a place of great power, a place where the malevolent force had once been bound. Alex knew that he had to find this chamber and confront the darkness once and for all.

With determination burning in his veins, he retraced his steps through the moonlit corridors, the memories of his previous journeys through the mansion fresh in his mind. The clock tower beckoned him once more, its imposing presence a symbol of the mysteries that lay hidden within Havenwood.

As he ascended the familiar staircase to the top of the tower, he couldn't help but wonder what awaited him in the hidden chamber below. The air grew colder with each step, and the sense of unease that had haunted him since his return to the estate weighed heavily on his shoulders.

Finally, he emerged onto the balcony, the moonlight illuminating the clock tower's intricate gears and mechanisms. But this time, he did not linger on the balcony. He was on a mission, driven by a relentless need to confront the malevolent force that had plagued his family for centuries.

With careful fingers, he examined the stone floor, searching for any sign of a concealed entrance. Then, he noticed it—a faint seam in the stone, barely visible in the dim light. It was the entrance to the hidden chamber.

As he pushed against the stone floor, it gave way with a soft rumble, revealing the staircase that led downward into the depths of Havenwood. He descended with lantern in hand, the shadows closing in around him, and the air grew colder with each step.

Finally, he emerged into the vast underground chamber, its walls adorned with ancient symbols and carvings that pulsed with an eerie light. In the center of the chamber stood the stone pedestal, upon which rested the book of forbidden knowledge. It was the same book that he had sealed away, and it seemed that the malevolent force had found a way to return.

With a sense of grim determination, Alex approached the stone pedestal, his voice steady as he began to chant the counter-incantation that had banished the darkness before. The chamber trembled, and the symbols on the walls glowed with an otherworldly light.

But this time, the malevolent force fought back with a furious intensity. Shadows swirled around the chamber, and the air crackled with dark energy. It was a battle of wills, a confrontation between the guardian of the estate and the darkness that sought to consume it.

As the battle raged on, Alex could feel his strength waning, the malevolent force pressing down upon him with a relentless force. But he refused to yield. He continued to chant, his voice unwavering, his will unbroken.

And then, in a burst of blinding light, the darkness was banished once more. The book of forbidden knowledge lay closed on the stone pedestal, its dark power vanquished. The malevolent force had been driven from Havenwood once and for all.

Exhausted but victorious, Alex stepped away from the stone pedestal, his breath ragged. The battle had been fierce, but he had emerged victorious. The malevolent force that had haunted his family for generations had been banished, its power sealed away.

As he left the underground chamber and ascended the narrow staircase, he couldn't help but feel a profound sense of relief. The battle against the darkness had come to an end, and Havenwood Manor stood as a sanctuary of peace once more.

The mansion itself seemed to breathe a sigh of relief, its grand corridors bathed in the soft light of dawn. The secrets of Havenwood had been unveiled, and the malevolent force that had plagued the estate had been vanquished.

With a weary but contented heart, Alex made his way through the mansion, knowing that the battle for the legacy of Havenwood had finally come to an end. The ghosts of the estate had whispered their secrets in the silence, and he had confronted the darkness and emerged victorious.

The morning outside was bright and filled with promise, a new day dawning over Havenwood Manor. Alex stood for a moment, gazing out at the sprawling estate, where the past and the present converged in a timeless dance.

With a sense of fulfillment, he turned and made his way back into the heart of the mansion. The legacy of Havenwood had been safeguarded, and the battle against the malevolent force was a battle that would never be fought again.

The Legacy's End

Months had passed since the final confrontation in the hidden chamber beneath the clock tower. Havenwood Manor had been shrouded in a peaceful stillness, and the oppressive atmosphere that had once plagued the estate had lifted. It seemed that the malevolent force that had haunted the Winters family for generations had been banished once and for all.

Alex Winters had settled into a semblance of a normal life within the mansion's grand walls. He had embraced his role as the guardian of the estate's secrets, and he had taken on the task of documenting the chronicle of Havenwood—a task that had been passed down through generations of his family.

The grand library had become his sanctuary, its shelves filled with books and manuscripts that told the story of Havenwood's complex history. It was there, among the tomes of knowledge and the flickering candlelight, that Alex poured over the pages of his grandfather's journal and the chronicle of secrets, piecing together the legacy of the estate.

One evening, as he sat at his desk in the library, a sense of unease settled over him—a feeling that something was amiss. He couldn't quite put his finger on it, but he knew that the past had a way of resurfacing, and the secrets of Havenwood were not so easily buried.

With a furrowed brow, he closed the chronicle of secrets and stood up, his footsteps echoing in the silence of the library. He made his way through the moonlit corridors of the mansion, the shadows dancing on the walls as if whispering their secrets.

As he entered the grand dining room, a chill ran down his spine. The candelabrum, once transformed into a beacon of light, had grown dim, its crystal drops losing their ethereal radiance. It was a stark contrast to the rest of the mansion, where the atmosphere remained peaceful and serene.

Alex approached the candelabrum with caution, his fingers tracing the cold crystal drops. He knew that the malevolent force had once been bound to this very object, and its dimming could only mean one thing—the darkness was returning.

With a sense of urgency, he began to examine the candelabrum closely, searching for any sign of tampering or sabotage. It was then that he noticed it—a faint etching on one of the crystal drops, a symbol he had seen before in his grandfather's journal.

As he touched the symbol, a surge of dark energy coursed through him, and the candelabrum sprang to life with an otherworldly radiance. Shadows danced on the walls, and a sense of malevolence filled the room.

Alex knew that he had stumbled upon a clue, a piece of the puzzle that hinted at the return of the malevolent force. But how had it managed to escape its prison in the hidden chamber beneath the clock tower?

With a sinking feeling, he realized that there must be another way into the underground chamber—one that had remained hidden from him. The darkness was resourceful, and it had found a way to infiltrate the mansion once more.

Determined to confront the malevolent force head-on, Alex retraced his steps through the mansion, his mind racing with thoughts of how to seal away the darkness once and for all. He couldn't allow the legacy of Havenwood to be tainted by the malevolent force any longer.

His search led him back to the clock tower, where he examined the balcony and the stone floor for any sign of a concealed entrance. But this time, the hidden passage remained elusive, as if mocking his efforts.

With frustration building, Alex returned to the grand library, determined to find answers. He scanned the books and manuscripts, searching for any reference to the hidden entrance to the underground chamber. It was then that he stumbled upon a handwritten note tucked within the pages of a dusty tome.

The note bore his grandfather's distinctive handwriting and contained a cryptic message: "The heart of Havenwood holds the key." It was a riddle, a clue left behind by Victor Winters to guide his descendants.

Alex's mind raced as he tried to decipher the message. The "heart" of Havenwood could mean many things—the central core of the estate, the place where the malevolent force had first taken root. But what was the "key" that would unlock the entrance to the underground chamber?

As he pondered the riddle, he realized that the answer was right before him—the candelabrum in the grand dining room. It had once been the source of the malevolent force's power, and now it held the key to sealing it away once more.

With newfound determination, Alex made his way to the dining room, the candelabrum still bathed in its eerie radiance. He reached out and touched the crystal drop with the etched symbol, and the darkness surged once more.

But this time, Alex was prepared. With a resolute mind and a heart filled with determination, he chanted the counter-incantation he had used in the underground chamber. The candelabrum's radiance intensified, and the shadows in the room seemed to recoil.

As the malevolent force struggled against the incantation, Alex could feel its power waning. With a final surge of energy, he uttered the last words of the incantation, and the candelabrum's light blazed with blinding intensity.

When the light finally faded, the candelabrum had been transformed. Its crystal drops now glowed with a pure and brilliant light, and the malevolent force had been sealed away once more.

Exhausted but triumphant, Alex knew that the battle was finally over. The legacy of Havenwood had been safeguarded, and the malevolent force that had haunted his family for generations had been banished for good.

As he left the dining room and made his way through the mansion, he couldn't help but feel a profound sense of relief. The secrets of Havenwood had been unveiled, and the malevolent force that had once plagued the estate had been vanquished.

The night outside was calm and still, the moon casting a silvery glow over the grand facade of Havenwood Manor. Alex stood for a moment, gazing up at the clock tower, where his journey had taken him time and time again. It was a place of mystery and malevolence, where the past and the present converged.

With a sense of finality, he turned and made his way back into the heart of Havenwood. The legacy of the estate had come to an end, and the darkness that had once haunted it was a memory that would fade with time.

www.ingramcontent.com/pod-product-compliance
Lightning Source LLC
LaVergne TN
LVHW050027080526
838202LV00069B/6943